THE USBORNE
ROUND THE WORLD
COOKBOOK

Caroline Young

Designed by Carol Law

Illustrated by Nadine Wickenden

Additional illustrations by Barry Jones
and Annabel Spenceley

Cookery consultant: Sarah Barrass
With special thanks to Julia Kirby-Jones

Food around the world

This book takes you on a worldwide tour of food, cooking and eating traditions. You will find out how to make some of the world's most famous dishes for yourself and how to serve them in the local style. The list below tells you which recipes from each country are in the book. The stars on the map show where the countries are.

1 USA

Pages 6-7
Pancakes
Hamburgers
Banana milkshake

2 Latin (South) America

Pages 8-9
Refried beans
Guacamole
Tacos
Tomato salsa

3 Caribbean

Pages 10-11
Mango ice-cream
Banana bread

4 Africa

Pages 12-13
Peanut bread
Bobotie

5 Spain and Portugal

Pages 14-15
Gazpacho
Sardine salad
Paella

6 France

Pages 16-17
Salade niçoise
French apple tart

7 The British Isles

Pages 18-19
Irish stew
Scones

8 Italy

Pages 20-21
Pizza Margherita
Spaghetti bolognese

9 The Netherlands

Pages 22-23
Cauliflower in cheese sauce
Fruit tarts

10 Germany

Pages 24-25
'Heaven and Earth'
Lebkuchen

11 Central Europe

Pages 26-27
Hungarian goulash
Dumplings
Sachertorte

12 Scandinavia

Pages 28-30
Smörgåsbord
Jansson's temptation
Red fruit pudding
Poor knights
Smørrebrød

13 Switzerland

Page 31
Raclette
Muesli

14 Greece and Turkey

Pages 32-33
Shish kebabs
Moussaka

15 Middle East

Pages 34-35
Hummus
Tabbouleh
Halva

16 Russia

Pages 36-37
Russian salad
Beef Stroganoff

17 China

Pages 38-39
Sweet and sour spare ribs
Fried rice with vegetables.

18 India

Pages 40-41
Bhuna gosht
Dhal
Cucumber raita

19 Japan

Pages 42-43
Vegetable casserole
Dipping sauce

20 Indonesia

Page 44
Chicken in coconut sauce

21 Australia and New Zealand

Page 45
Lamingtons

Jewish cooking

Pages 46-47
Cheesecake
Potato latkes

Canada

USA

Caribbean

South America

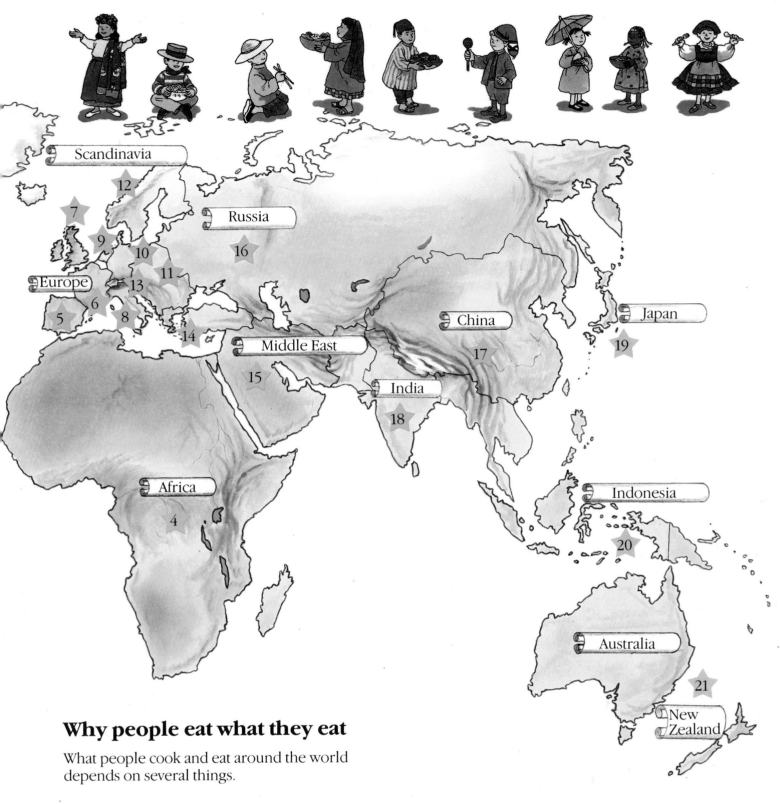

Scandinavia

12

7

Russia

9

10

16

11

Europe

13

5   6

8

China

Japan

14

19

Middle East

15

India

18

17

Africa

4

Indonesia

20

Australia

21

New Zealand

Why people eat what they eat

What people cook and eat around the world depends on several things.

The weather in different places affects which crops farmers grow. The ones they grow most are the cheapest to buy locally. A country's traditional dishes are usually made with these local foods.

Coconuts grow well in Indonesia, so are used in many local dishes.

In some poor countries, if the weather spoils the main crop, people have no food. They may starve unless richer countries can send some.

Wealthy countries can afford to buy foods from all over the world. There are many more different things for people to choose to eat.

Exotic fruit and vegetables from the Caribbean or Africa are found in European supermarkets.

Some people choose not to eat certain things. Vegetarians do not eat meat and vegans don't eat meat, fish or dairy foods (butter, cheese and so on). A religion may forbid certain things. Muslims and Jews do not eat pork, for example.

Before you start

The tips and hints on this page will help you enjoy your cooking and make sure you get the very best results. Read them all the way through before you start.

First of all

Before you try any recipe in this book, read it right through. If there's anything you don't understand, ask. Then do these things before you start.

Wash your hands well, tie back long hair and put an apron on.

Make sure the kitchen surfaces are clean and clear.

If you're told to, turn the oven on. For a fan oven, reduce the heat as the manual says.

Get all the ingredients you will need measured out.

Wash any fruit and vegetables thoroughly in cold water.

Put an oven shelf in the right place:
Over 190°C (375°F)/Gas mark 5 – high
Over 160°C (325°F)/Gas mark 3 – middle
Below this temperature – low
Put it anywhere in a fan oven.

Safety first

Some things you do when you cook can be dangerous. Always follow these simple rules in the kitchen.

● Never start cooking without an adult in the kitchen.

● When you see this symbol in the book, take extra care.

● Be very careful when slicing or chopping with sharp knives.

● Turn pan handles to the side so that you can't knock them over.

● If you spill anything on the floor, mop it up straight away.

● Take great care when you are frying food, or using hot water.

● Have a heatproof mat or chopping board to put hot dishes onto.

● Wear oven gloves to lift things in and out of the oven.

● Never leave the kitchen when gas or electric rings are on.

● If you can, wash up dirty dishes as you go, to clear space.

About measuring

Ingredients are measured in grams, litres and millilitres as well as pounds, ounces and pints in this book.

Just follow one set of measurements carefully.

Most recipes in this book are enough for four people to eat. You can multiply the ingredients for more people, or divide them for fewer.

'1 tbs' means one tablespoonful. It should be flat, or level, across the top, not heaped.

'1 tsp' means one level teaspoonful.

A *'pinch'* of something means about the amount that you can pinch between your thumb and your forefinger.

Cookery tips

Here are some tips you will find useful as you cook some of the recipes in this book.

Separating an egg

Gently crack the egg on the edge of a bowl. Pull the shell apart, keeping the egg in one half. Carefully tip the yolk from one half to the other a few times so the white drops into the bowl. Slide the yolk into a cup if it's not needed right away.

Heating fat

Cooking oil, butter, margarine and lard are all types of fat. You need to take great care when heating fat as it gets very hot quickly and can spit and catch fire. Only heat it until a faint, shimmery haze rises above the pan.

Watery eyes

Onions and spring onions can make your eyes water when you chop them. Try rinsing these vegetables in cold water before you start chopping them up.

Greasing tins

To stop food sticking in a tray or tin, wipe it all over inside with kitchen towel dipped in margarine, and line the base with greaseproof paper. Place the tin on the paper and draw around it for the shape.

Cookery words

Here are some words used in cookery that you may find in this book. Check what they mean here if you are not sure when you read them in a recipe.

Cream: mix fat and sugar into a cream with a wooden spoon or electric mixer.

Rub in: mixing fat and flour by rubbing them with your fingertips.

Beat: mix together by stirring very hard with a wooden spoon or electric mixer.

Fold in: mix two things using a gentle, slicing movement with a metal spoon.

Simmer: cook over a low heat, so that the food or water bubbles gently.

Blend: make something into a smooth paste, usually in an electric blender.

Fry: cook in a little hot fat (oil, butter, lard or margarine).

Whisk: add air by beating very fast with a hand whisk. (Or use an electric one.)

Bring to the boil: cook at a high heat, until the food or water bubbles.

Knead: squeeze and stretch dough to make it ready for baking.

Sift/sieve: pass dry ingredients through a sieve to get any lumps out.

The United States of America

The United States of America, or USA, is made up of 50 states. About 300 years ago, people from all over the world went to settle in this huge country. They took recipes from their homelands with them, so American cooking is made up of lots of different styles. Here are two recipes that are popular all over the USA today.

Pancakes

Traditional American pancakes are quite small and thick. They are often called flapjacks. People eat them for breakfast with bacon and eggs or with sweet maple syrup. This mixture makes about ten pancakes.

The United States is one of the world's most important farming countries. This map shows what American farmers produce. They grow all sorts of fruit, grain and vegetables. Some keep huge herds of cattle for beef as well.

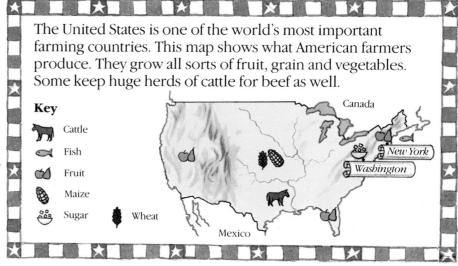

Key
- Cattle
- Fish
- Fruit
- Maize
- Sugar
- Wheat

Canada
New York
Washington
Mexico

You will need:

150g/5oz plain flour	*3 tbs vegetable oil*
2 tsp baking powder	*300ml/¹/₂ pint milk*
pinch salt	*maple syrup, maple-flavour*
1 egg	*syrup, golden syrup or warmed jam*

1. Sieve the flour, baking powder and salt into a medium-sized mixing bowl.

2. In another bowl, whisk the egg, 2 tbs of the oil and the milk together.

3. Beat this liquid into the flour. Cover the bowl with cling wrap and refrigerate for half an hour.

4. Pour the last 1 tbs of oil into a frying pan. Heat it until a faint haze rises from the pan.

Make them about 10cm (4ins) wide.

5. Using a ladle, slowly pour two or three small pools of pancake mixture into the pan.

6. When the pancakes bubble, flip them over and cook the other side. Serve them straight away.

Slow syrup

Maple syrup comes from the sap of maple trees. Each tree only produces about two bottles of syrup in a whole year.

Maple syrup is quite expensive. Maple-flavoured sauce is cheaper and tastes just as good.

Thanksgiving

On 28th November 1621, some early American settlers cooked a turkey to thank God for their first harvest. Today, this day is a holiday called Thanksgiving. Americans still cook turkey to celebrate it.

Hamburgers

The first hamburgers were made in Hamburg, Germany. German settlers probably first took the recipe to America, but American cooks have made hamburgers famous around the world.

You will need:

500g/1lb lean minced beef
1 small chopped onion
pinch salt and pepper
1 tbs vegetable oil

4 soft bread rolls
2 tomatoes
4 lettuce leaves

1.

Put the beef, onion, salt and pepper into a mixing bowl. Gently squeeze them into a ball with your fingers.

2.

Divide this ball into four equal balls. Pat them into a burger shape 1cm (½ in) thick and the same size across as your rolls.

If you can, keep the rolls warm in an oven that's just on.

3.

Cut the rolls into two flat halves. Grill the insides until they are lightly browned, then lay the rolls out on a plate.

Pastry brush

4.

If you plan to grill your burgers (see next step), brush both sides with oil on kitchen paper or a pastry brush.

Make sure they don't burn.

5.

You can fry burgers in oil, or put them under a hot grill, or grill them on a barbecue. Cook each side for five minutes.

6.

While the burgers cook, wash the lettuce and tomatoes and dry them with kitchen paper. Slice up the tomatoes and gherkins.

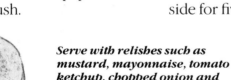

Serve with relishes such as mustard, mayonnaise, tomato ketchup, chopped onion and dill pickles.

7.

Put a lettuce leaf, some tomato and a burger onto the bottom half of each roll. Put a top half on top and press gently.

Banana milkshake

Milkshakes go well with hamburgers. Here's how to make a fresh banana milkshake for one.

You will need:

300ml/½ pint milk
1 chopped banana

Put the milk and the banana in a blender for about two minutes. Pour into a tall glass and serve with a straw. You could add a scoop of vanilla ice cream, too.

Latin America

All the land between Mexico and the bottom of Argentina is known as Latin America. The main cooking ingredients of these countries are tomatoes, hot chilli peppers and beans, often served in pancakes made from maize flour. Some recipes were first made by tribes of Indians who lived in Latin America centuries ago, such as the Aztecs, Mayas and Incas.

Latin America contains mountain ranges, rainforests, plains called pampas, lush valleys and steamy swamps. Farmers use the land in lots of different ways. They grow many crops and keep beef cattle.

United States of America

Mexico

Mexico City

Peru

Lima

Brazil

Rio de Janeiro

Chile

Argentina

Buenos Aires

Key

Cattle

Cocoa

Coffee

Fruit

Maize

Sheep

Tropical fruit

Wheat

Refried beans

Latin American cooks use beans in lots of different ways. Here, cooked, canned beans are mashed and then cooked again in a frying pan.

You will need:	*1 clove of garlic, peeled*
1 400g/14oz can kidney beans	*pinch of salt*
1 medium onion	*30g/1oz lard or margarine*
	60g/2oz grated cheese

1.

Peel and chop the onion. Crush the garlic clove with a fork or in a garlic crusher.

2.

Melt the fat in a frying pan until a haze rises. Fry the onions and garlic until soft.

3.

Mash the drained beans into the mixture with a fork. Fry them until fully hot, then serve.

Sprinkle on the salt and grated cheese just before you eat.

Tacos

Tacos are crisp maize pancakes stuffed with meat, fish, salad and tasty toppings such as guacamole and refried beans. Lots of shops now sell tacos that just need baking for two minutes before you fill them yourself.

1.

Here are some ideas for cooked meat or fish to put in the bottom of tacos.

Fry 250g (½lb) of minced beef, a little chopped onion, salt and pepper for about 15 minutes.

Try mixing a can of tuna with a little lemon juice and salt and pepper. Add some mayonnaise if you like.

You could chop two cooked chicken breasts into very small pieces. Add salt and pepper and lemon juice.

Guacamole

Guacamole is a creamy mixture made from avocado pears. The Aztecs probably made it first, 500 years ago. You can eat it on its own as a spicy dip, or as a filling in tacos (see below).

Use an electric blender if you can.

1. Stone

Cut the avocados in half longways around the stone. Pull the halves apart and take out the stone. Scoop the flesh into a bowl.

2. Add all the other ingredients to the avocado. Mix in a blender, or with a fork or potato masher, until the mixture is quite smooth.

3. Pour your guacamole into a bowl. Serve it as soon as you can, as it goes brown if you leave it for too long.

These tortilla chips, made from maize flour, are delicious dipped in guacamole. Many shops sell them.

Salsas

In Latin America, people serve hot, spicy sauces, called salsas, with many meals. Some salsas are made with so much fresh chilli that they can actually burn your mouth.

Tomato salsa

You will need:

2 tomatoes, peeled (see page 14)
1 small onion
1 tsp chilli powder
pinch salt and pepper
2 chopped parsley sprigs
pinch sugar

Chop the tomatoes and onions. Mix all the ingredients together and serve in a bowl. Add more chilli powder if you like really hot flavours.

Tomato salsa is crunchy and mild.

A variety of salsas may be on the table at once, for people to choose from.

2. Cut strips of lettuce and slices of tomato. Put them on top of the meat or fish.

3. Spoon some refried beans and guacamole into each taco. Top with grated cheese.

The Caribbean

The Caribbean is made up of more than 20 islands. Over the centuries, many different peoples have lived on them. Each one planted their own crops and cooked them in different ways. Today, Caribbean food is an exciting mixture of several cooking styles. It is often known as Creole cooking. These two recipes use two of the many exotic Caribbean fruits.

Mango ice-cream

Mangoes are delicately-flavoured fruit that grow in the Caribbean. Many supermarkets sell fresh mangoes. Delicatessens and health food shops sell them in cans. Here, they are made into ice-cream.

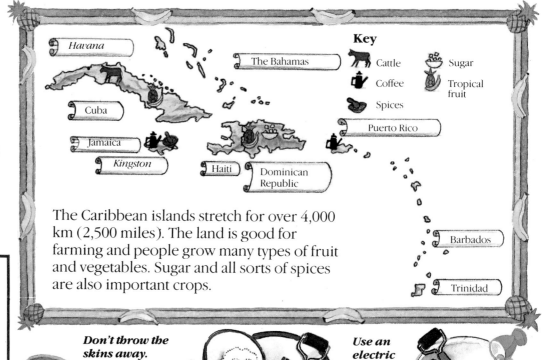

Key

- Cattle
- Coffee
- Spices
- Sugar
- Tropical fruit

Havana
The Bahamas
Cuba
Jamaica
Kingston
Haiti
Dominican Republic
Puerto Rico
Barbados
Trinidad

The Caribbean islands stretch for over 4,000 km (2,500 miles). The land is good for farming and people grow many types of fruit and vegetables. Sugar and all sorts of spices are also important crops.

You will need:

4 eggs, separated (see page 5)
120g/4oz caster sugar
300ml/½ pint double cream
2 mangoes or 2 medium cans of mango pulp
1 tsp lemon juice

Turn the control knob on your freezer to 'maximum' before you start. Turn it up after step 6.

Don't throw the skins away.

1. Empty the canned pulp into a bowl, or cut both fresh mangoes in half and dig out their flat stones. Scoop the flesh into a bowl.

2. Whisk the egg whites until you can pull blobs up with your whisk to stand up in points. Add the sugar and whisk for two more minutes.

Use an electric whisk if you can.

3. In another bowl, whisk the cream until it is quite thick. Add the egg yolks one by one, whisking the mixture a little after each one.

4. Making small, gentle cutting movements with a metal spoon, add the cream mixture to the egg whites. Don't stir too hard.

Set an alarm clock to go off in 1½ hours to remind you.

5. Add the mashed mango and lemon juice in the same way as step 4. Pour it all into a tub with a lid. Freeze with the lid on for 1½ hours.

6. Scoop the mixture into a bowl and whisk it for two minutes. Pour it back into the tub and freeze until it is solid, as ice cream should be.

Don't forget to turn your freezer up when the ice cream is ready.

Try serving your ice cream in the hollowed-out mango skins.

Banana bread

Bananas are an important food in the Caribbean. People cook and eat them in many different ways. You can eat this banana bread buttered, or with some cream, as a pudding.

You will need:

120g/4oz butter or margarine
90g/3oz caster sugar
90g/3oz brown sugar
1 egg
250g/8oz wholemeal flour
2 tsp baking powder
pinch salt
pinch nutmeg
1 tsp vanilla essence
2 large bananas
90g/3oz raisins
90g/3oz chopped walnuts
2 tbs milk

 Set the oven to 180°C(350°F)/ Gas mark 4

Fantasy islands

When the explorer Christopher Columbus first saw the islands of the Caribbean, he thought he had reached Paradise because they were so beautiful.

1.
Cut the butter into cubes. Using a wooden spoon, cream the butter and all the sugar together until smooth.

This is hard work at first.

2.
Sieve the flour, baking powder, nutmeg and salt into another bowl. Add the raisins and nuts and stir well.

If the mixture goes lumpy, stir in a spoonful of the flour mixture.

3.
In a cup, beat the egg and the milk together with a fork. Beat them into the butter mixture bit by bit.

4.
Make slicing movements with a metal spoon to mix the flour mixture gently into the butter and egg mixture.

5.
Peel the bananas and mash them with a fork. Add the vanilla essence to them, and stir them into the main mixture.

6.
Grease and line (see page 5) a 1 pint loaf tin. Pour the mixture in and smooth the top with a knife.

7.
Bake your banana bread for about one hour, or until a skewer comes out clean when you stick it into the loaf.

8.
Run a blunt knife between the loaf and tin. Put a wire rack on the tin and turn both over. Tap to make the loaf drop.

Exotic fruits

Some of the most exotic fruit and vegetables in the world grow on the islands of the Caribbean. Today, you can see many of them in our supermarkets. Here are some to try.

This fruit is a papaya or pawpaw. It is delicious with lemon juice.

Caribbean cooks use a lot of sweet, white coconut flesh and its see-through milk.

This fruit is called an ackee. People say it tastes like scrambled egg.

Caribbean farmers grow a lot of pineapples. They send them all around the world.

Put your bread in a tin when it is cool, to keep it fresh.

Africa

Africa is made up of more than 40 separate countries. Each one has its own traditional dishes, but cooking styles are similar. African cooks have to use whatever crops grow nearby, so they cook different sorts of food in different parts of this huge continent.

There are deserts, mountains, swamps, plains and jungles in Africa. Farmers grow whatever they can in each area. In some places, so little rain falls that it is difficult to grow enough food for everybody.

Cairo
Morocco
Algeria
Libya
Egypt
Sudan
Ehtiopia
Addis Adaba
Zaire
Kenya
Nairobi
Tanzania
Johannesburg
South Africa

Key

Cattle		Sheep	
Citrus fruit		Sugar	
Cocoa		Tropical fruit	
Maize		Wheat	

Peanut bread

Peanuts, or groundnuts, are an important crop in many parts of Africa. Here, they are made into a sort of bread. It will keep for days in a tin with a lid.

You will need:

60g/2oz unsalted shelled peanuts
375g/12oz plain flour
3 tsp baking powder
30g/1oz caster sugar
pinch salt
1 egg
300ml/½ pint milk

Set the oven to 180°C(350°F)/ Gas mark 4

1.

Chop the peanuts in a blender or put them in a plastic bag and roll a rolling pin over them.

2.

Sieve the flour, salt and baking powder into a mixing bowl. Using a fork, beat the egg in a cup.

18cm (7in) wide
28cm (11in) long
4cm (1½in) deep

3.

Stir the beaten egg, sugar, milk and peanuts into the flour. Spoon into a greased baking tray.

4.

Smooth the top and leave for 20 minutes. This makes the cooked bread a lighter and more even texture.

5.

Bake the bread for half an hour until golden. When cool, cut squares to eat with cheese or jam.

Bobotie

This is a traditional dish in South Africa. People from all over the world have settled there. The food they make today shows this, as it mixes so many different flavours.

You will need:

500g/1lb minced beef
2 slices bread
30g/1oz butter
300ml/½ pint milk
1 onion, chopped
1 garlic clove, crushed
60g/2oz dried apricots, chopped

60g/2oz flaked almonds
60g/2oz raisins
½ tsp chilli powder
1 tsp curry powder
2 tbs lemon juice
2 eggs
pinch salt and pepper

 Set the oven to 170°C(325°F)/ Gas mark 3

1.
Rip the bread into pieces. Put it in a shallow dish and pour half the milk over it. Leave it to soak.

2.
Melt the butter in a frying pan. Fry the meat, onions and garlic for about five minutes, stirring all the time.

3.
In a bowl, mix the curry and chilli powders, lemon juice, salt and pepper. Stir in the meat mixture bit by bit.

4.
Add the nuts, raisins, apricots and soaked bread. Stir in any milk that is left in the dish the bread soaked in.

5.
Press the hot mixture into an ovenproof dish. Whisk the two eggs and the rest of the milk. Pour them over the top.

6.
Bake your bobotie for one hour. The egg and milk will set like a golden custard. Serve it straight away.

Spices, such as chilli and curry powder, were first used in Africa to hide the taste of meat that had gone bad in the hot climate.

African vegetables

In Africa, cooks make vegetables into dumplings or pastes called fufus. They make a meal more filling, as rice, potatoes or bread do in other countries.

This is a cassava root. It can be dried, ground and made into dumplings.

Plantains are a large, green sort of banana. They can be made into dumplings, too.

Yams are peeled and softened in hot water. People make them into fried yam balls.

Maize is made into maize flour. When mixed with water, it makes a mashed paste called ugali.

13

Spain and Portugal

The traditional dishes of these two countries tell a fascinating story. Around 500 years ago, Spanish and Portuguese sailors conquered South America and lands in the East. They brought back food that people at home had never seen before, such as tomatoes, peppers and new spices. Cooks in Spain and Portugal mixed these ingredients with ones that grew at home in recipes such as these.

Gazpacho

This tangy Spanish soup is called gazpacho. It is very refreshing as it is served ice cold. It was probably first made out of bits of leftover salad.

You will need:

6 spring onions	1 green pepper	pinch salt and
6 ripe tomatoes	1 slice of bread	pepper
½ a cucumber	2 tbs olive oil	120ml/¼ pint very
1 clove of garlic, peeled	2 tbs wine vinegar or lemon juice	cold water

1. Cut the crusts off the bread. Crumble the bread into a saucer. Add the vinegar or lemon juice. Leave it to soak into the bread.

⚠️ *The skins should peel off easily.*

2. To skin the tomatoes, lower them into a bowl of boiling water for two minutes, then into one of cold water for two minutes.

3. Chop the onion, pepper, cucumber and peeled tomatoes. Crush the peeled garlic clove in a crusher or with a fork.

4. Put the vegetables and soaked bread in a blender for three minutes, or push them very hard through a sieve with a spoon.

5. When the mixture is smooth, add 120ml (¼ pint) cold water. Pour your soup into a serving bowl. Stir in the olive oil.

Sardine salad

Portuguese cooks use a lot of fish. Here, sardines are made into a tasty starter.

You will need:

4 lemons	2 tomatoes,
2 cans sardines	chopped
2 tbs vinegar	4 black olives
	salt, pepper

1. Cut the top third off each lemon. Scoop the flesh into a bowl. Mix the sardines, salt, pepper and vinegar with it.

2. Spoon 1 tbs chopped tomato into each lemon case. Fill them up with the sardine mixture and put a black olive on top.

In Spain, gazpacho is often served with bowls of chopped fresh vegetables, like these.

6. Sprinkle with salt and pepper. Cover the bowl with cling wrap and put in the refrigerator for an hour before serving.

Paella

This dish, called paella, is a whole meal in itself. Spanish cooks believe that food should look as good as it tastes, so try to make your paella really bright and colourful.

The sun ripens fruit, olives, nuts and grapes for wine in Spain and Portugal. There is plenty of fish to catch, too, as they are surrounded by the sea on three sides.

You will need:

1 medium onion
1 red pepper
1 small can tomatoes
1 clove of garlic
2 skinned chicken breasts
1 chicken stock cube
450ml/3/4 pint boiling water

250g/8oz long grain rice
120g/4oz prawns
60g/2oz frozen peas
2 tbs vegetable oil
1 tbs saffron or turmeric
pinch salt and pepper

To decorate:

6 fresh mussels
1 lemon
sprig of fresh parsley

1.

Chop the onions, red pepper, and tomatoes into small pieces. Peel and crush the garlic clove with a fork or crusher.

2.

Slice the chicken. Heat the oil in a large frying pan that has a lid. Fry the chicken until it goes white on the outside.

3.

Add the onion, garlic, salt and pepper. Fry them until they are quite soft. Add the tomatoes to the pan and stir well.

4.

Pour the boiling water onto the stock cube in a jug. Stir it until dissolved. Carefully pour the stock into the pan.

5.

If the rice sticks, add a little more water.

Add the rice and stir in the saffron or turmeric. Put the lid on the pan and cook over a low heat for about 15 minutes.

6.

If any mussels don't open, they are bad. Throw them away.

Stir in the prawns and peas. Arrange the mussels on top and cook your paella for five more minutes with the lid on.

7.

Cut a lemon into wedges. Arrange them on top of the paella. Sprinkle with some parsley and serve hot.

Favourite fish

Dried cod is a Portuguese speciality. Each fish is sprinkled with salt and dried for several months before it is cooked.

Paella is often cooked and served in a pan like this. It is called a paellera.

15

France

France is famous for food and cooking. The French for a cook is 'chef de cuisine', which means 'head of the kitchen'. Many important cooking techniques came from French chefs.

In France, lots of people enjoy spending a long time cooking and eating meals. These two French dishes will not take too long to make, but look good and taste delicious.

Salade niçoise

This colourful fish salad was first made in the city of Nice, in the south of France. It is called 'salade niçoise', which means 'salad from Nice'.

You will need:

2 eggs
4 tomatoes
1 lettuce
1 green pepper

1 small can French beans
1 medium can of tuna, drained
1 can anchovies
a few black olives
sprig of fresh parsley

The yolks go grey if you don't do this.

1.
Boil the eggs for ten minutes. Then plunge them into cold water. When cool, tap and peel off their shells.

2.
Wash the lettuce and gently dry it with kitchen paper. Arrange the leaves in the bottom of a big salad bowl.

3.
Sprinkle on the beans. Slice the pepper and cut three tomatoes into quarters. Arrange them around the bowl.

4.
Make a mound of tuna in the middle of the salad. Pour the oil off the anchovies and lay them over the top.

5.
Decorate with slices of hard-boiled egg and olives. Top with slices of the fourth tomato and parsley.

French dressing

Some people add a sauce to salad, called a dressing. The simplest dressing is called 'vinaigrette', or French dressing. It was first made in France.

You will need:

4 tbs olive oil
4 tsp vinegar
1 tsp mustard
(French is best)
pinch caster sugar
pinch salt and pepper

Pour all the ingredients into a jar with a screw-on top. Put the top on and shake hard. Pour the mixture over the salad just before serving.

Truffle-hunters

In France, pigs and dogs are trained to sniff out especially tasty mushrooms, called truffles. They grow under the ground. Good ones are very expensive.

French apple tart

France is famous for its pastries and cakes. Shops called 'patisseries' sell them. This tart recipe comes from northern France, where farmers grow a lot of apples.

1.

Peel the green apples and cut them into quarters. Cut out the core bits and slice the quarters up quite thinly.

2.

Put the apples in a pan with 2 tbs water. Cook them over a low heat until soft (about five minutes). Stir with a wooden spoon.

You will need:

180g/6oz plain flour
90g/3oz butter or margarine, cut into cubes
60g/2oz caster sugar
1 egg
3 green eating apples
3 red eating apples
2 tbs apricot jam

 Set the oven to 200°C(400°F)/ Gas mark 6

Keep rubbing until the mixture looks like crumbs.

3.

Sieve the flour into a bowl. Add the butter cubes and rub them between your fingertips in the bowl of flour.

Add a couple of drops of water if it too dry to stick together.

4.

Separate the egg (see page 5). Add the sugar and the egg yolk to the flour mixture and squeeze it gently into a ball.

Push the rolling pin away from you. Turn the board if you need to.

5.

Sprinkle some flour onto a board and a rolling pin. Roll the pastry until it is about 26cm (10in) wide and 2cm (1in) thick.

If the pastry breaks, press it in a piece at a time.

With a fork, prick the case all over.

6.

Line a 20cm (9in) flan dish with pastry. Trim the edges and put in the refrigerator for 30 minutes. Then bake for five minutes.

Make the slices overlap, like this.

7.

Take the pastry out of the oven. Spoon in the cooked apples. Slice the red apples, dip in lemon juice and lay them in circles on top.

France is the biggest farming country in Europe. It sends food such as cheese, fruit and vegetables all over the world. French grapes are used to make wine, too.

Key

- Cattle
- Fish
- Fruit
- Grapes
- Pigs
- Sheep
- Vegetables
- Wheat

British Isles
Belgium
Germany
Paris
Switzerland
Bordeaux
Italy
Nice
Spain

8.

Mix the jam with 2 tbs hot water and spread it over the apples. Bake your tart for about 30 mins, until golden on top.

The British Isles

There are five countries in the British Isles. They are England, Scotland, Ireland, Northern Ireland and Wales. Each country has its own traditional dishes, but cooking styles are similar everywhere. Here are two well-known British recipes for you to try.

Irish Stew

Stew is a mixture of meat and vegetables. It is cooked for a very long time to make the meat tender and blend all the flavours together. This tasty stew recipe is from Ireland.

You will need:

750g/1½lbs lamb (cubed stewing lamb or neck or shoulder joints)
750g/1½ lbs old potatoes
2 large onions

1 tsp mixed herbs
1 meat stock cube
450ml/¾ pint boiling water
pinch salt and pepper

 Set the oven to 170°C(325°F)/ Gas mark 3

1.

If you are using a lamb joint, cut it into cubes 2cm (1in) big, on a chopping board. This is quite tricky, so ask for help.

2.

Peel the potatoes and cut them into slices about 1cm (½in) thick. Peel and chop the onions into small pieces.

Use a dish with a lid.

3.

Cover the bottom of a large dish with meat cubes. Add a layer of onions, then put a layer of potato slices on top.

Make the top layer potato slices.

4.

Carry on adding layers of meat, onions and then potatoes until the dish is full. Sprinkle with the herbs, salt and pepper.

5.

In a jug, dissolve the stock cube in the boiling water. Slowly pour the stock liquid into the dish and put the lid on.

6.

Put the dish on a baking sheet to catch spills. Cook the stew for about two hours. After one hour, add some water if it looks dry.

Sunday lunch

Traditionally, lunch on Sunday is roast meat and vegetables in the British Isles.

With roast lamb, people serve a sauce made from mint leaves and vinegar. Apple sauce comes with roast pork. With roast beef, cooks make a mixture of eggs, milk and flour called Yorkshire pudding.

In Ireland, a dish called Colcannon is often served with Irish Stew. It is made of mashed potatoes and boiled cabbage.

Scones

Scones are small cakes. People often split them in half and spread them with butter, jam or cream. This recipe makes about 12 scones.

You will need:

250g/8oz self-raising flour
60g/2oz butter, cut into cubes
60g/2oz caster sugar

4 tbs milk
pinch salt

 Set the oven to
220°C(425°F)
Gas mark 7

Farming land is limited in the British Isles. Fruit, vegetables and grain grow on the best land. Sheep and cows graze in fields and on moors and hills.

Scotland
Edinburgh
N. Ireland
Belfast
Dublin
England
Wales
Ireland
Cardiff
London

Key

Deer   Sugar
Cattle   Wheat
Sheep   Potatoes
Fish   Fruit

1.
Sift the flour into a mixing bowl to get rid of any lumps. Add the pinch of salt.

2.
Rub the butter cubes into the flour with your fingertips until the mixture is like breadcrumbs.

Add 1 tsp of water if it is too dry to stick together.

3.
Add the sugar and milk and gently squeeze the mixture into a ball with your fingers.

4.
Roll the mixture out on a floured board until it is about 1.5cm (¾in) thick.

5.
Cut circles out of the mixture with a round cutter or a cup. Put them onto a greased baking tray.

6.
Bake your scones for about ten minutes, until brown on top. Leave them to cool on a rack.

Tasty seaweed

In South Wales, people cook a seaweed called laver that they collect on the beach. They mix it with oatmeal and fry it. Then, it is called laverbread.

This kind of thick cream is called clotted cream.

Cut your scones in half like this.

Tea in the British Isles is often a meal of scones with other cakes and cups of tea, served in the late afternoon.

Italy

Italy has been famous for its cooking since the Ancient Romans ruled there, over 2,000 years ago. Today, people all over the world eat some traditional Italian dishes, such as spaghetti bolognese and pizza. In Italy, cooks take great care choosing and cooking their ingredients.

Pizza Margherita

Pizzas were first made in the southern Italian city of Naples. They can have many different toppings. This one was named after the first Italian queen, Margherita. It takes about 1½ hours to make, so start cooking well before you want to eat.

You will need:

250g/8oz strong bread flour
1 tbs/½oz dried yeast
or use 'easy-blend' yeast, as the packet says
1 tbs sugar
150ml/¼ pint warm water
400g/14oz can tomatoes
2 tbs tomato purée
60g/2oz grated cheese
½ tsp dried oregano
pinch salt and black pepper

You can serve pizza hot or cold.

A crisp salad goes well with slices of pizza.

Try putting other toppings, such as fried onions, grilled bacon bits, olives, peppers, mushrooms, sweetcorn, pineapple, or tuna onto your pizza base.

1. Mix the sugar and dried yeast with 2 tbs warm water in a small bowl. Leave in a warm place for 10-15 minutes or until it goes light and frothy on top.

Pull the mixture in from the sides of the bowl with your fingers.

2. Sieve the flour and salt into another bowl. Make a hollow in the middle and pour in the yeast and the rest of the warm water. Gently squeeze into a ball.

This is called kneading.

3. On a floured board, stretch the dough out, then fold it over. Press down on it with your palm, turn the dough around and do the same movements again.

The dough will grow to double its size.

4. When the dough is soft and stretchy, put it in a bowl covered with a cloth in a warm place for an hour. After 45 minutes, set the oven to 230°C(450°F)/Gas mark 8.

Press with your palm.

5. Knead the risen dough a little more. On a greased baking tray, press it into a round shape about 1cm (½in) thick and 30cm (12in) wide.

6. Pour away the juice from the canned tomatoes. Chop them up in a bowl. Stir in the tomato purée, oregano, salt and black pepper.

7. Spread the tomato mixture evenly over the pizza base. Sprinkle with grated cheese and cook for about 25 minutes, until golden on top.

Spaghetti Bolognese

Pasta

In the colder north of Italy, farmers grow wheat and keep cows for milk and cheese. Further south, fruit, grapes for wine, and vegetables ripen in the hot summer sun.

Switzerland

Austria

Parma

Venice

Bologna

Key

Rome

Naples

Cattle

Citrus fruit

Fish

Grapes

Olives

Sugar

Sicily

Bolognese sauce was first made in the city of Bologna, in northern Italy. It is traditionally served on top of spaghetti.

You will need:

500g/1lb minced beef
3 rashers bacon, cut into strips 2cm (1in) wide
1 medium onion, chopped
1 medium carrot, chopped
60g/2oz mushrooms, sliced
1 clove of garlic, peeled and crushed
1 medium can tomatoes
2 tbs tomato purée
90g/3oz butter
½ tsp dried oregano
½ tsp dried basil
salt and black pepper
375g/12oz spaghetti

Spaghetti is one of over 50 sorts of Italian pasta. Pasta means 'dough' or 'paste' in Italian. It is made of flour, eggs and salt mixed together. It should be cooked 'al dente', which means soft but not soggy.

Pasta sheets are called lasagne. Cooks put meat between layers of lasagne, with sauce on top.

These pasta tubes are called macaroni. They are often served in cheese sauce.

Pasta can be made into fancy shapes, like these.

This pasta has some wholemeal flour in it.

If spinach is added to pasta, it is called 'pasta verde', which means 'green pasta' in Italian.

These pasta envelopes are called ravioli. They are stuffed with meat.

Make sure you use a pan that has a lid.

1. Melt half the butter. Fry the bacon, garlic, onion, carrot and mushrooms in it for three minutes.

2. Add the beef and cook it until it browns. Add the tomato purée, canned tomatoes, basil and oregano.

3. Add 4 tbs water and simmer the sauce for 20 minutes, with the lid on. Stir it quickly after ten minutes.

⚠️

4. Boil 750ml (1½pints) of water in a pan. Put the spaghetti ends in, then slowly push it all in as it softens.

5. Boil the spaghetti for about eight minutes. Then tip it into a colander over the sink to drain it.

Eating spaghetti

Eating spaghetti is tricky. Try winding it around a fork. Use a spoon to stop it slipping off the bottom.

Make a sauce with tomatoes and vegetables if you are vegetarian.

6. Lift the spaghetti onto four plates, using two forks. It's quite slippery, so doing it quickly is best. Add the rest of the butter and spoon on some bolognese sauce.

Italians sprinkle grated cheese from the town of Parma onto spaghetti. It is called Parmesan.

21

The Netherlands

The Netherlands is also called Holland, and people from here are known as Dutch. Food in the Netherlands is simple and wholesome. It is a very flat country, so icy cold winds blow right across it in winter. Many traditional Dutch recipes were first made to warm people up on cold days.

Cauliflower in cheese sauce

Holland is famous for its cheeses. Here, cheese is made into a hot, creamy sauce to pour over vegetables. Use a Dutch cheese, such as Gouda or Edam, if you can.

1.

Take the leaves off the cauliflower and cut it into four. Cook in boiling water for ten minutes, then drain at once.

2.

Melt the butter in a pan. With a wooden spoon, stir in the flour, salt and pepper to make a smooth paste. Cook for one minute.

Cheese races

Some Dutch towns hold weekly cheese markets. It is a tradition for cheese carriers to race each other to see who can carry their load the fastest.

3.

Off the heat, gradually stir in the milk. Back on the heat, bring the sauce to the boil, stirring all the time. Then turn the heat off.

4.

Stir in most of the grated cheese. Drain the cauliflower and tip it into a heat-proof dish. Pour the cheese sauce over it.

5.

Sprinkle on the rest of the cheese. Put the whole dish under the grill until the top starts to bubble and goes brown.

Try serving thick slices of brown bread and butter with this dish.

Fruit tarts

This recipe for fruit tarts comes from the city of Limburg, in the southern Netherlands. The tarts have a bread base, so they take some time to make, but they are delicious.

Spicy banquet

Rijstaffel, (which means 'rice table' in Dutch), is a banquet of up to 25 different dishes served with rice. Dutch traders brought the recipes back from the islands of Indonesia when they went there in the 1700s.

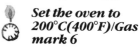

Set the oven to 200°C(400°F)/Gas mark 6

1.

Mix the dried yeast with the milk and 1 tbs of the sugar in a small bowl. Leave in a warm place until the yeast goes frothy.

2.

Melt the butter in a pan. Take it off the heat. While it cools in the pan, sieve the flour, the rest of the sugar and salt into a large mixing bowl.

3.

Pour the warm butter and yeast into the flour. Gently squeeze into a ball. Knead the dough (see step 3, page 20).

4.

Cover the bowl and leave it in a warm place for an hour. Then divide the risen dough into four balls, about ½cm (¼in) thick.

The sea could easily flood the flat land of the Netherlands. Windmills pump any water off the land and walls hold back the sea. Dutch farmers grow vegetables, bulbs and flowers to send all around the world. They keep cows for milk and cheese, too.

Germany

Amsterdam
The Hague
Rotterdam

Key

🐄 Cattle
🌷 Flowers
🍎 Fruit
🐖 Pigs
🥬 Vegetables

Belgium

Sprinkle with a little more sugar if you like.

5.

Put the dough balls onto a baking tray. Cut open the fresh or canned fruit and take out any stones. Arrange the fruit on the dough.

6.

Cook your tarts for 20 minutes, then turn the oven down to 180°C (350°F)/Gas mark 4 for ten more minutes. Eat them hot or cold.

Germany

Germany is well-known for certain sorts of food and drink. You can buy German sausages, such as frankfurters, in many countries today. Germany is also famous for its beer and white wine.

Cakes and biscuits are another speciality. Typical German dishes are quite simply flavoured, but very tasty. Here are two recipes that give you an idea of their style of cooking.

'Heaven and Earth'

This dish is often called 'Heaven and Earth' because it is made of apples, (which grow up in the sky) and potatoes, (which grow in the earth). It is popular as a hot lunch or supper.

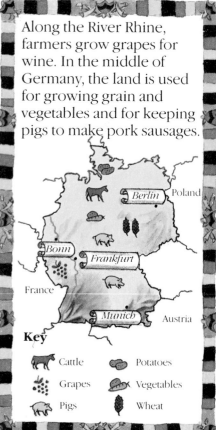

Along the River Rhine, farmers grow grapes for wine. In the middle of Germany, the land is used for growing grain and vegetables and for keeping pigs to make pork sausages.

You will need:

750g/1½lbs potatoes
750g/1½lbs cooking apples, peeled and with the cores cut out

2 medium onions
8 frankfurters (in a can or a packet)
2 tbs caster sugar
30g/1oz butter
pinch salt and pepper

1. Peel and slice the potatoes. Put them in a pan that has a lid. Cover with water and add a pinch of salt. Boil them with the lid on for 15-20 minutes, until soft.

2. Slice the apples and put them in another pan. Add 2 tbs water and cook the apples over a low heat until they are soft (about five minutes). Then add the sugar.

3. Cook the frankfurters as the can or packet tells you to. They can usually be grilled, fried or put in hot water for five minutes.

4. Peel and slice the onions. Melt the butter in a frying pan and fry the onions until they are soft and slightly brown around the edges.

Use a spoon to press them over to one side.

5. Pour the water from the potatoes and mash them with pepper. Spoon them into one half of a casserole (a deep, oven-proof dish).

Frankfurters were first made only in the German city of Frankfurt.

6. Spoon the apples into the other half of the dish. Arrange the cooked frankfurters on top, spoon on the fried onions and serve straight away.

Gingerbread house

In Germany, they celebrate the Feast of Saint Nicholas on 6th December. Children are given lots of cakes, biscuits, fruit and sweets. Sometimes, they get a small house made of gingerbread, like this.

Lebkuchen

These spicy biscuits are often called Lebkuchen. This means 'love biscuits' in German. In south Germany, it is a tradition for lovers to give each other heart-shaped Lebkuchen. People also decorate them and hang them on Christmas trees. This mixture makes about 15 biscuits.

You will need:

4 tbs clear honey
60g/2oz butter or margarine
250g/8oz plain flour
1 tsp baking powder
60g/2oz brown sugar
30g/1oz cocoa

2 tsp dried ginger
1 tsp mixed spice
1 egg
90g/3oz icing sugar
1 tbs lemon juice

Set the oven to 200°C (400°F)/ Gas mark 6

1.
Put the honey, sugar and butter in a pan over a low heat, until the butter melts. Take the pan off the heat and leave to cool.

See page 5 for how to separate an egg.

2.
Sieve the flour, baking powder, cocoa, ginger and spice into a bowl. Add the egg yolk. Keep the egg white aside.

Add a few drops of water if it won't stick together.

3.
Use a metal spoon to mix the warm honey, butter and sugar into the flour. With clean hands, squeeze the mixture into a ball.

4.
Roll the mixture out on a floured board until it is ½cm (¼in) thick. Cut some shapes out with pastry cutters or a knife.

5.
Make a hole at the top of each biscuit with a skewer. Lift them onto a greased baking tray and bake them for about ten minutes.

Shallow, oblong, metal tray.

6.
Let the biscuits cool on a wire rack. Sieve the icing sugar into a bowl. Mix in 2 tsp of egg white to make icing.

7.
Add food colouring if you want, then spoon some icing into an icing bag. Slowly squeeze the bag over each biscuit, making any pattern you like with the icing.

You can use a cone of greaseproof paper, with a small hole cut in one corner, instead of an icing bag.

8.
When the icing decoration is dry, you can thread ribbons through the holes in the top of your Lebkuchen and hang them up, or eat them straight away.

25

Central Europe

The countries between Germany in the west and Russia in the east are often called Central Europe. Winters here are very cold, so thick soups and stews fill people up and keep them warm. Rich, creamy cakes are a speciality, too.

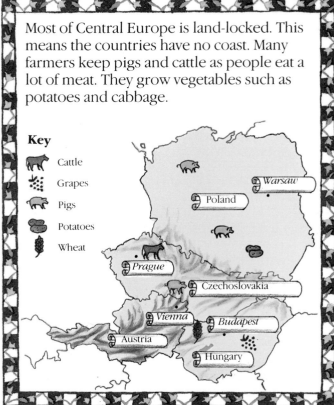

Most of Central Europe is land-locked. This means the countries have no coast. Many farmers keep pigs and cattle as people eat a lot of meat. They grow vegetables such as potatoes and cabbage.

Key
Cattle
Grapes
Pigs
Potatoes
Wheat

Warsaw
Poland
Prague
Czechoslovakia
Vienna
Budapest
Austria
Hungary

Hungarian goulash

Goulash is named after the Hungarian word 'gulyas', which means shepherd. Shepherds are supposed to have invented this dish. It has hot paprika in it, which is made from red peppers.

You will need:

500g/1lb stewing beef, cut into cubes
1 large onion, chopped
4 large potatoes, chopped
1 tbs cooking oil
2 tbs paprika
1 medium can tomatoes

1 clove garlic, peeled and crushed
1 beef stock cube
450ml/³/4 pint boiling water
pinch salt and black pepper
small carton sour cream or natural yogurt

1. Heat the oil in a large pan that has a lid. When a faint haze rises from it, fry the beef cubes until they are brown. Stir in the chopped potatoes.

2. Add the onion, garlic, tomatoes, paprika, salt and pepper to fry. Dissolve the stock cube in the boiling water and pour it in. Stir everything well.

3. Cook your goulash with the lid on for about an hour, over a low heat. Serve it hot with a dollop of sour cream or natural yogurt on top and some rice or bread.

Dumplings

Central European cooks often add small dumplings made of dough to stews. They make the dish more filling.

You will need:

90g/3oz self-raising flour
1 egg
pinch salt

Mix all the ingredients together. Drop small balls of dough into your goulash ten minutes before serving.

Hungarians often eat rye bread, like this, with goulash.

Sachertorte

This rich chocolate cake was first made in 1832, by the cook Franz Sacher. He baked it for an Austrian prince. Its name means 'Sacher's cake' in German.

You will need:

150g/5oz margarine
150g/5oz caster sugar
250g/½lb block plain chocolate
6 eggs, separated (see page 5)
120g/4oz plain flour sieved
150/5oz apricot jam
2 tbs butter
250g/8oz icing sugar
30g/1oz cocoa

Set the oven to 170°C(325°F) Gas mark 3

See-through strudels

The best-known Austrian cakes are apple strudels. Cooks make the strudel pastry so thin that you can read a newspaper through a single sheet of it, people say.

1.

Mix the margarine and sugar together with a wooden spoon until they are soft and creamy. Beat in the egg yolks one by one.

Wear an oven glove to lift the hot bowl.

2.

Put half the chocolate, broken into cubes, in a bowl over a pan of boiling water. When it melts, add it to the mixture.

Always use a clean whisk.

3.

In another bowl, whisk the egg whites until you can pull blobs with the end of your whisk into peaks that stand up.

4.

With a metal spoon, fold in the sieved flour, one spoonful at a time. Then fold in the egg whites in the same way.

5.

Pour into two greased and lined cake tins, 20cm (8in) wide. Bake for 35 minutes, or until a skewer stuck in comes out clean.

6.

Run a blunt knife around between the tin and cake. Turn the tin over onto a wire rack and tap it to make the cake drop out.

7.

Melt the rest of the chocolate (see step 2). Mix into a paste with the butter and 1 tbs of the icing sugar. Spread it over one cake half.

8.

Put the two halves together. Stir the jam well, then spread it in a thin layer all over the top and sides of the cake with a knife.

Don't make the icing too runny.

9.

Sieve the rest of the icing sugar and the cocoa into a bowl. Add water until the mixture drops from a spoon as you count to three.

10.

Smooth the icing all over the top and sides of the cake. Leave it to harden before you slice it up.

Serve your Sachertorte with whipped cream.

Sweden, Norway and Finland

Sweden, Norway, Denmark, Finland and Iceland make up Scandinavia. You can find out about Denmark and its food on page 30.

Smörgåsbord

Sweden is most famous for its smörgåsbord, which means 'bread and butter table'. The smörgåsbord is a selection of salads, fish dishes, hot food, puddings and breads laid out on a big table. Here are two typical smörgåsbord dishes.

Jansson's temptation

This tasty dish is called Jansson's temptation. It was probably named after a Swedish opera singer called Pelle Janzon, who loved it.

You will need:

500g/1lb potatoes, peeled
2 large onions, chopped
2 cans anchovies, drained
60g/2oz butter

300ml/½ pint milk
pinch salt and pepper

Set the oven to 400°F(200°C)/ Gas mark 6

Scandinavia is often known as the 'Land of the Midnight Sun'. This is because, during its short summers, the sun shines all day and all night.

A lot of Scandinavia is covered with forest. Denmark has the best farming land. The long, jagged coastlines are excellent for fishing, though.

Iceland
Reykjavik
Russia
Norway
Finland
Sweden
Oslo
Helsinki
Stockholm
Denmark
Copenhagen

Key:
Cattle
Fish
Pigs
Reindeer
Wheat

1. Cut the potatoes into thin strips 2cm (1in) wide and 4cm (2ins) long. Put a layer in a quite small, but deep, pie dish.

2. Cover the potato layer with one of anchovies, then one of chopped onions. Repeat to the top of the dish.

3. Finish off with a layer of potato strips. Add salt and pepper and pour the milk over the top of it all.

4. Put small blobs of butter over the dish. Bake it for about 45 minutes, until it is crisp and brown.

Christmas crown

December 13th, or St Lucia's Day, is the beginning of Christmas in Sweden. Young girls dress in white, wear a crown of candles and give out buns and wine.

Red fruit pudding

Fruit ripens quickly in the short Scandinavian summer. People make special fruit puddings, like this, to celebrate Midsummer. This recipe is from Norway.

You will need:

500g/1lb/2 medium cans raspberries, blackcurrants or redcurrants, or a mixture of all three

2 tbs caster sugar
2 tbs cornflour
450ml/³/₄ pint cold water or juice from the canned fruit
some flaked almonds

1.

Put the fruit, sugar and water or juice in a pan. Cook over a low heat for five minutes to soften the fruit. Leave to cool.

2.

Push the fruit mixture through a sieve into a bowl. Use a metal spoon. Throw away any bits that won't squeeze through.

3.

In a cup, mix the cornflour with a spoonful of the fruity liquid. Stir this mixture into the fruit.

Stir it with a wooden spoon all the time.

4.

Pour the fruit mixture back into the pan and bring it to the boil. Lower the heat and cook for five minutes.

5.

When cool, pour the fruit into bowls. Sprinkle with the nuts and chill for 30 minutes in the refrigerator.

You could serve a jug of cream with your fruit pudding.

Poor knights

This recipe for a sweet snack comes from Finland.

You will need:

2 eggs
300ml/¹/₂ pint milk
pinch cinnamon
8 slices bread
30g/1oz butter
60g/2oz caster sugar

1.

In a bowl, beat the eggs, milk and cinnamon together. Stir in half the sugar.

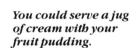

2.

Trim the crusts off the bread. Soak the slices in the milk mixture for five minutes.

Fry two or three slices at a time.

3.

Melt the butter in a frying pan. Fry the slices of bread until golden on both sides.

4.

Sprinkle your poor knights with the rest of the sugar. Serve with jam or fruit and cream.

29

Denmark

Denmark is part of Scandinavia, but the sea separates it from Norway, Sweden and Finland. It is famous for the bacon and cheese it produces.

These traditional open sandwiches make a tempting, colourful spread for lunch or a snack.

Smørrebrød

Danish open sandwiches are called smørrebrød, which means 'buttered bread' in Danish. To make them, just lay the ingredients onto a slice of buttered bread. Eat them with a knife and fork.

Prawns and lemon

Put a lettuce leaf on the bread. Spoon on some prawns. Top with a lemon twist (see below) and black pepper.

Salami and tomato

Cover the bread with overlapping slices of salami. Add two slices of tomato and some onion rings (see below).

Cheese and tomato

Lay slices of cheese on top of the bread. Put a row of overlapping tomato slices up the middle.

Cheese and anchovy

Cover the bread with slices of cheese. Add criss-crossed strips of anchovy and some onion rings (see below).

Lettuce and egg

Put a lettuce leaf on the bread. Cover with overlapping slices of hard-boiled egg and a little cress.

Twists and twirls

Delicious, sticky cakes are a Danish speciality. Other people call them Danish pastries, but the Danes call them 'Viennese bread'. They come in many shapes and sizes.

Decorating smørrebrød

Here are some ideas for making your smørrebrød colourful and attractive.

1.

Make a small cut up the middle of a slice of lemon. Twist it like this so it stands up.

2.

Slice a gherkin lengthwise several times almost down to the end. Spread the slices out like a fan.

3.

You could slice across the top of an onion to make rings. Also try cress, parsley or chopped spring onions.

Switzerland

Switzerland is right in the middle of Europe. People speak four different languages, depending on what part of the country they live in. They are French, Italian, German and Romansh.

Raclette

The two best-known Swiss cheeses are called Emmenthal and Gruyère. Traditionally, people held the whole cheese on a fork in front of a fire to melt some for this dish. It's easier to melt slices of cheese under a grill, though.

The Alps mountains cover most of Switzerland. Cows graze on the grassy slopes. They produce the creamy milk that makes Swiss chocolate and cheese.

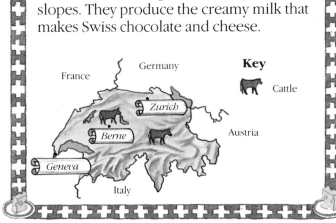

France
Germany
Key
Zurich
Cattle
Berne
Austria
Geneva
Italy

You will need:

4 medium potatoes
250g/8oz cheese (Swiss, if you can get some)

1.

Scrub the potatoes, but do not peel them. Boil them until a knife comes out easily when stuck in (about 15 minutes).

2.

Cut the potatoes in half. Lay slices of cheese over the flat side and grill them until the cheese melts.

Swiss people serve raclette with pickled onions.

Children eat raclette in a famous Swiss children's book, called 'Heidi'.

Muesli

Muesli is a mixture of grains, such as oats, with fruit and nuts. It was first made in 1897 by a Swiss doctor called Bircher-Brenner, as a healthy breakfast food. Change the amounts of each ingredient to suit your taste.

The word muesli comes from the German word muësli, which means 'mixture'.

For each person:

1 tbs rolled oats
1 tbs wheat flakes
1 tbs barley flakes
6 tbs water
1 tbs chopped mixed nuts
1 tbs dried fruit
2 tbs lemon juice
1 apple
1 tbs honey
milk

1.

In a bowl, soak the oats, wheat and barley in the water before you go to bed at night. This will soften them.

2.

Next morning, peel and grate the apple. Add the lemon juice to prevent it going brown. Stir it into the soaked grains.

3.

Add the dried fruit and as much milk as you want. Top with the spoonful of honey and the nuts.

Greece and Turkey

People eat similar sorts of food in Greece and Turkey, but both countries have specialities. Some of them, such as kebabs, are popular in many countries today. Some traditional recipes were first written down over 2,000 years ago, by the Ancient Greeks.

Shish kebabs

In this Turkish recipe, cubes of lamb are cooked on metal skewers to make shish kebabs. This means 'roast meat stuck on a skewer'. Serve them in pitta bread (bought at a delicatessen) with salad. This recipe makes eight kebabs.

You will need:

750g/1½lbs lamb, cut into cubes
4 tbs olive oil
4 tbs lemon juice
½ tsp oregano
½ tsp rosemary
pinch salt and pepper
8 lettuce leaves
4 tomatoes
½ a cucumber
8 pitta breads

1.
Mix the oil, 3 tbs of the lemon juice, oregano, salt and pepper in a bowl. Soak the meat cubes in this mixture for one hour.

2.
Wash the lettuce and dry it with kitchen paper. Cut the leaves into strips. Cut the tomatoes into quarters and slice the cucumber.

Mind the sharp skewer point.

3.
Push about six cubes of meat onto each skewer. Leave a little gap between each cube. Sprinkle them with a little rosemary.

Wear oven gloves. The skewers will be hot.

4.
Grill the kebabs under a hot grill for about ten minutes. Keep turning them to make sure they cook all the way through.

5.
Warm the pitta breads quickly under the grill. Carefully slice each one along the top and open it up, like an envelope.

6.
Put some salad into each pitta. Push the meat cubes off a skewer into each one. Sprinkle with the rest of the lemon juice.

Cakes and sweets

Greek and Turkish cakes and sweets are very sweet. Special cake shops sell them.

This is Turkish delight. It is made by boiling grapes into a jelly. Sometimes it is flavoured with roses.

This is a baklava. It is made of thin pastry called filo. It is filled with nuts, then soaked in honey.

This cake, called a kadeifi, is made from pastry that looks a bit like cotton threads. People often eat it with coffee.

You could serve your kebabs with rice instead of in pitta.

Moussaka

This delicious Greek dish traditionally uses minced lamb. You can use beef, though. If you are vegetarian, try a mixture of tomatoes, onions, courgettes and mushrooms instead.

You will need:

1 large aubergine	*pinch oregano*
500g/1lb minced lamb	*pinch salt and pepper*
1 large onion, chopped	*30g/1oz butter*
4 tbs olive oil	*1 tbs flour*
1 medium can	*1 egg*
tomatoes	*300ml/½ pint milk*
	60g/2oz grated cheese

A lot of land in Greece and Turkey is not good for growing crops. It is rocky and dry so sheep and goats graze on it. Olive and lemon trees grow well, though.

Key: Olives · Citrus fruit · Sheep · Grapes · Wheat

Set the oven to 190°C (375°F)/ Gas mark 5

Put the lid on to cook.

1. Slice the aubergine into 1cm (½in) slices. Heat 2 tbs of oil in a pan with a lid. Fry the onion and meat until browned. Add the tomatoes, oregano, salt and pepper. Cook for 30 minutes.

2. In a frying pan, heat the rest of the oil and fry each slice of aubergine until it is soft. Then flip it over and cook the other side. Do a few slices at a time. Add more oil if you need to.

3. Spoon half of the meat mixture into a casserole (deep, oven-proof dish). Cover it with a layer of aubergine slices. Repeat the layers with the rest of the meat and aubergines.

In Greece, this cheese is often added to salads. It is called feta.

4. In a small bowl, beat the egg. Melt the butter in a pan. Stir in the flour to make a smooth paste. Cook it for one minute. Keep stirring.

Stir the whole time.

5. Off the heat, stir the milk into the pan. Back on the heat, bring the sauce to the boil. Take it off again, cool slightly, then add the beaten egg.

Tasty tavernas

In Greece and Turkey, people often eat in restaurants called tavernas. Many are outside, with shady vines instead of solid roofs.

6. Pour the sauce over the casserole. Sprinkle your moussaka with grated cheese and cook it in the oven for about 45 minutes, until it is brown and crisp on top. Serve it hot with a fresh salad.

The Middle East

The area called the Middle East stretches from the top of Africa in the west across to the edge of Russia in the east. It includes 20 separate countries. Most people in Middle Eastern countries are Muslim, so they do not eat pork or drink alcohol. Families usually eat meals together, though it is traditional for people not to speak at all while they are eating.

Mezze

Many Middle Eastern meals begin with a selection of starters, which are called 'mezze'. Health food shops sell all the ingredients you need.

Hummus

This chickpea paste is called hummus. It makes a good snack or a tasty starter.

You will need:

250g/8oz dried chick-peas, soaked in water overnight, or
1 medium can chickpeas
1 clove of garlic, peeled and crushed
1 tbs light tabina (sesame seed paste)

6 tbs lemon juice
2 tbs olive oil
3 tbs milk
pinch salt and pepper

To decorate:
a sprig of fresh parsley

A lot of the Middle East is desert. Farmers grow fruit and vegetables such as chickpeas and lentils where enough rain falls. They keep sheep and goats, too.

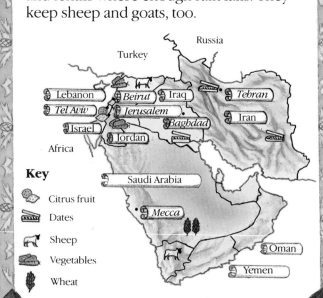

Keep an eye on the boiling chickpeas. Add more water if they dry up.

1.

Boil fresh chickpeas in water for two hours, or until soft. Drain the water and let them cool. If you are using canned ones, just pour away the water.

2.

Put four whole chickpeas aside. Put the rest into a blender, or push them hard through a sieve with a spoon. They will make a smooth paste.

3.

Mix in all the other ingredients. Put the whole chickpeas and the parsley on top. Serve your hummus with some warmed pitta bread (you need to buy this).

Tasty tea

Middle Eastern people shop in indoor markets called souks. In tiny tea shops, they can refresh themselves with glasses of mint tea.

Tabbouleh

This crunchy salad comes from Lebanon. It can be a snack or a starter (mezze). It uses a grain called burghul. People scoop it up with lettuce leaves to eat it in the Middle East.

You will need:

250g/8oz fine burghul
6 spring onions
3 tomatoes
1 green pepper
4 lettuce leaves

2 sprigs each chopped fresh parsley and mint or 2 tbs each if dried
6 tbs olive oil
6 tbs lemon juice
pinch salt and pepper

The spoon squeezes the water out of the grains.

1.
Soak the burghul in cold water for 15 minutes. Pour it into a sieve and push down with a spoon.

2.
Chop the spring onions and tomatoes. Cut out the pepper's core and seeds and chop it into small pieces.

Dry the lettuce on a tea towel or kitchen paper.

3.
Wash the lettuce leaves and pat them dry. In a small bowl, mix the oil, lemon juice, salt and pepper together.

4.
In a big bowl, mix up the burghul, vegetables, parsley and mint. Add the oil mixture and stir everything well.

5.
Put a lettuce leaf on each person's plate. Pile some tabbouleh on top and serve.

Halva

Halva is a type of sweet. There are many different sorts. A square of halva is often served at the end of a meal in the Middle East, with glasses of tea or strong coffee.

You will need:

90g/3oz caster sugar
120g/4oz butter
120g/4oz semolina
300ml/½ pint water
2 drops vanilla essence

To decorate:
about 20 blanched almonds (without their brown skins)

1.
Cook the sugar and water over a low heat until the sugar is dissolved. The water will go clear.

← *Keep stirring all the time.*

2.
Melt the butter in another pan. Add the semolina and cook for three minutes. Stir all the time. Add the vanilla essence.

3.
Off the heat, stir the sugary water into the semolina. Back on the heat, stir for three more minutes, until very thick.

4.
Tip it into a dish 25cm (10in) across and 1cm (½in) deep. Smooth the top and mark 5cm (2in) squares.

5.
Stick an almond in the middle of each square. Serve squares of cool halva with tea or coffee.

35

Russia

Russia is the biggest of the republics, or states, that made up what used to be called the Soviet Union. Together, they cover an area bigger than the whole of Europe. They all have their own cooking traditions, but while they were united, some recipes became popular throughout the region.

Russian salad

Vegetables are used to make all sorts of dishes in Russia. Here, they are cooked and made into a crunchy salad. Serve it as a starter, or as meal in itself. You can add some cheese, ham or tuna if you like.

You will need:

2 medium carrots
3 medium potatoes
90g/3oz peas (cooked frozen peas or tinned peas)
3 small, cooked beetroots
2 tbs mayonnaise
pinch salt and pepper
washed lettuce leaves to line the salad bowl
10 slices cucumber
1 hard-boiled egg (see page 16)

Most of this part of the world is very cold indeed in winter. Only potatoes, turnips and beetroots grow well under the frozen ground. In summer, farmers grow huge fields of grain, and sunflowers for their oil. It is difficult for them to grow enough food for everybody to eat.

Poland

St. Petersburg

Kiev   Moscow

Russia

Turkey

China

Iran

Key

Pigs   Vegetables

Cattle   Sugar   Wheat

Maize   Sunflowers

1. Peel the potatoes and carrots. Cook them for 15 minutes in a pan of boiling water with the lid on.

2. Pour the water off the vegetables and leave them to cool. Line a small dish with the washed lettuce leaves.

You can add some chopped cooked chicken or fish to your Russian salad if you like.

3. Chop the vegetables and beetroot into 1cm (½in) cubes. Tip them into a bowl. Add the peas, salt and pepper.

4. Stir the mayonnaise into the vegetables. Spoon them into the dish. Decorate with slices of cucumber and hard-boiled egg.

36

Easter eggs

In some places, children dye and decorate hard-boiled eggs to celebrate Easter. If you want to try it, you can buy egg dyes from craft shops or make your own with some of these vegetables.

Spinach dyes eggs green.

Onions give a rich brown.

These are some traditional Russian egg-patterns.

Beetroot dyes them red.

1.
Boil 250g (½lb) of the vegetable you choose for 20 minutes in a large pan of water. The water will change colour.

2.
Spoon the vegetables out of the pan. Boil the eggs in the coloured water in the pan for ten minutes.

3.
Let the eggs cool down. Dip a cocktail stick in vinegar or lemon juice and scratch a pattern onto the dyed egg.

Beef Stroganoff

This recipe was first made in the 1700s, for Count Alexander Stroganoff. You need expensive steak to cook it properly, so save it for special occasions.

You will need:

500g/1lb rump steak
60g/2oz butter
1 medium onion, sliced
120g/4oz mushrooms, sliced

150ml/¼ pint sour cream
1 tsp mustard
1 tsp salt and pepper

1.
On a board, cut the steak into strips about 1cm (½in) wide and 6cm (2½ins) long. Sprinkle them with salt and pepper and cover with kitchen paper.

2.
Melt the butter in a large frying pan. Add the onion slices and fry them until they are soft and see-through. Keep stirring them all the time.

3.
Add the sliced mushrooms and fry them for about two minutes. Stir in the mustard. Carefully lay the strips of steak around the frying pan. Mind your fingers.

4.
Cook your Stroganoff for about five minutes, moving the ingredients around the frying pan all the time. The steak will go brown on both sides.

5.
Turn the heat down and stir in the sour cream. Cook gently for another two minutes, then serve straight away with rice or flat noodles.

37

China

Chinese food is popular in many countries today. There are thousands of different Chinese dishes. Some more unusual recipes use ingredients such as chickens' feet, sharks' fins and birds' nests. But most Chinese people cook simpler dishes like the ones on this page.

 Sweet and sour spare ribs

Chinese recipes often combine different tastes, such as sweet and sour. This sauce adds a tangy taste to pork spare ribs.

You will need:

1.5kg/3lbs meaty pork spare ribs
1 small onion, chopped
1 clove of garlic, peeled and crushed
1 tbs grated fresh ginger, or 1 tsp dried ginger

3 tbs vegetable oil
pinch salt
2 tbs sugar
2 tbs vinegar
1 tbs soy sauce
1½ tbs tomato purée
2 tbs orange juice

1.
Rinse and pat dry the spare ribs. Cut off as much of the fat as you can. Sprinkle them with a little salt.

2.
Pour the sugar, vinegar, soy sauce, tomato purée and orange juice into a deep casserole dish. Stir them well.

3.
Put the ribs in the sauce, cover and leave them for about an hour. They will soak up the flavours in the sauce.

⚠️ *Cook your ribs a few at a time. Keep them warm under the grill.*

4.
Heat the oil in a frying pan. Fry the ribs for about five minutes, stirring them all the time as they cook.

5.
Turn the heat down a bit and add the onion, garlic, ginger and the sauce from the casserole dish.

6.
Fry for about ten more minutes, until the pork is crisp. Keep stirring the ribs around the pan so that they do not burn.

Stir-frying

Chinese food is often fried over a high heat in a pan called a wok. The first woks were used over 5,000 years ago in China. Food is stirred all the time, so this way of cooking is called stir-frying.

7.
Lift the ribs onto plates and spoon the sauce in the pan over them. It's best to eat them with your fingers.

You could serve spare-ribs as a starter, or with some rice as a main course.

Fried rice with vegetables

Chinese people cook rice in lots of different ways. For this recipe, You need to cook it as the packet tells you before you start.

You will need:

375g/12oz cooked rice
6 mushrooms
150g/5oz bean sprouts
6 iceberg lettuce leaves
(ask for this kind of
lettuce in the shop) or
Chinese leaves, if you
can get them
120g/4oz frozen peas

6 spring onions
1 garlic clove, peeled
and crushed
1 tsp grated fresh
ginger or 1 tbs, if dried
3 tbs soy sauce
3 tbs vegetable oil
(groundnut or sesame
oil is best)

China is huge and over a billion people live there. Farmers plant rice, wheat and maize. They also keep cattle, pigs, chickens and ducks for their meat.

Russia

Key

Cattle

Citrus fruit

India

Ducks

Rice

Fish

Pigs

Maize

Wheat

Peking

Shanghai

Hong Kong

1.
Slice the mushrooms. Cut the lettuce leaves into thin strips. Slice the spring onions into 2cm (1in) slices with your knife at a slant.

2. ⚠
In a frying pan, heat the oil until a haze rises. Add the garlic and ginger and fry for 30 seconds. Stir them all the time.

3.
Add the mushrooms and fry for two minutes. Stir in the spring onions, peas, lettuce, rice and bean sprouts. Keep everything moving.

4.
Sprinkle on the soy sauce and stir-fry (fry and stir all the time) for five more minutes. If the rice starts to stick, add 2 tbs of water. Serve at once.

You can add prawns, bits of cooked chicken, or tuna to fried rice at step 3, if you like.

How to use chopsticks

Chinese people eat with chopsticks. If you want to have a go at using them, you might find it tricky at first, so keep practising.

Slot the thick end of one chopstick in the hollow between your thumb and first finger.

Rest the middle firmly on your third finger.

Hold the second chopstick between your thumb and your first finger, as you would hold a pen.

Move your first finger and thumb to lift the top chopstick up and down. The ends will pinch together to pick up food.

India

Cooking styles in India are very different from one area to another. What people can cook and eat depends on their religion, too. Indian cooks are expert at blending spices to create delicious flavours in their dishes.

Thali

Most Indian meals are made up of several dishes. Often, each dish is served in a small metal bowl called a 'katori'. The katoris are all laid on a tray called a 'thali', so meals like this are called 'thalis', too. Rice is usually put in the middle.

Bhuna gosht

Indians do not use the word curry. People from the West gave Indian dishes this name. The mixture of spices makes each Indian dish different. This one is made of lamb and tomatoes.

Over 300 million people live in India. Growing enough food is difficult, so most land has to be farmed in some way. Grain, rice, tea and spices are the main crops.

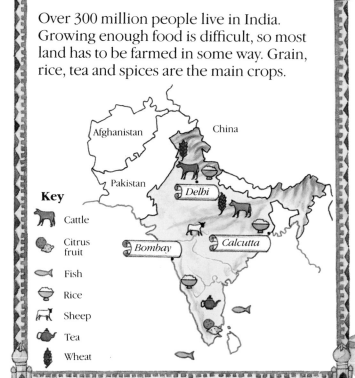

You will need:

750g/1½lbs lean lamb
1 onion, chopped
2 cloves garlic, peeled and crushed
60g/2oz butter
3 tomatoes, quartered
1 medium can tomatoes
4 tbs lemon juice
1 meat stock cube plus 300ml/½ pint boiling water
pinch salt
1 tsp chilli powder
2 tsp ground coriander
2 tsp black pepper
1 tsp ground cumin
1 tsp turmeric

Basmati rice

The best rice for Indian dishes is basmati rice. Cook about 60g/2oz of rice for each person. Follow the instructions on the packet or box.

1.
Melt the butter in a frying pan. Fry the onion and garlic for about five minutes, until they are soft.

2.
Cut the lamb into 2.5cm (1in) cubes. In a bowl, sprinkle them with salt and lemon juice. Leave to soak for 15 minutes.

3.
Stir the spices, pepper, onion and garlic into the lamb. Add the tomatoes and pour into a deep pan.

4.
Dissolve the stock cube in the boiling water and add it to the pan. Let your bhuna gosht bubble gently for an hour.

5.
Taste your bhuna and stir in a little more chilli powder if you like spicy food. Serve hot with some rice.

40

Dhal

Dhal is the Indian word for pulse vegetables such as lentils and beans. Over 50 different sorts of dhal grow in India. Cooks make them into a spicy sauce, which is also called a dhal.

You will need:

250g/8oz red lentils
pinch chilli powder
1 clove garlic, crushed
1 small onion, chopped

60g/2oz butter
1 tsp turmeric
450ml/¾ pint water
pinch salt
1 tsp ground cumin

Wash the lentils and pick out any stones.

Add more water if they start to stick.

1. Melt the butter in a deep pan. Fry the garlic and onion for about three minutes, until they are soft.

2. Add the turmeric, chilli powder, lentils and water. Bring to the boil, stirring all the time.

3. Turn the heat down and let the mixture bubble for about 20 minutes. The lentils will go soft and mushy.

4. Off the heat, stir in the salt. Pour your dhal into a serving bowl and sprinkle with a little ground cumin.

Cucumber raita

Raitas are made of yogurt mixed with fresh vegetables and herbs. They cool your mouth down after spicier dishes.

You will need:

300ml/½ pint thick natural yogurt
½ a cucumber
pinch each salt, black pepper
2 tbs chopped fresh mint (or dried mint)

Black pepper

1. Peel the cucumber and slice it lengthways, from top to bottom. Now cut the slices into strips about 3cm (1½ins) long.

2. Mix the cucumber strips with all the other ingredients in a bowl. Cover with cling wrap and put in the refrigerator for 30 minutes.

Making masalas

The mixture of freshly-ground herbs and spices in an Indian dish is called a masala. Curry powder is a ready-made masala, but it is not as good as a fresh one.

This is turmeric. It colours food yellow and adds a spicy flavour.

These cumin seeds have quite a strong, scented taste.

These are cardamom pods. They have a fresh taste.

Black pepper

Ginger

Coriander adds a delicate perfume as well as taste.

Mustard seeds add hot, peppery flavour to any dish.

Chilli powder

Black pepper, ginger, cloves, nutmeg and chillis go into masalas, too.

Nutmeg

Cloves

Japan

Food in Japan is some of the healthiest in the world. It is beautifully presented as well. The Japanese eat a lot of fish, vegetables, noodles and rice. It can be difficult to get exactly the right Japanese ingredients, such as dried seaweed and fish. The ones suggested here give you a taste of their cooking. Health food shops sell all the things you need to make this meal.

Japan is made up of four main islands. Mountains cover a lot of land, so farming is difficult. People grow rice, vegetables and fruit on good land. Some farmers breed fish and grow seaweed for food in underwater farms.

China

Tokyo

Osaka

Fish

Key

Rice

Citrus fruit

Vegetables

Vegetable casserole

Traditionally, people make this dish in the winter in Japan. Arrange the vegetables attractively in the dish to look really Japanese.

> **You will need:**
>
> *3 medium carrots*
> *4 spring onions*
> *4 mushrooms*
> *3 cabbage leaves*
> *1 medium potato*
> *150g/5oz tofu (soya bean curd)*
>
> *1 vegetable stock cube*
> *600ml/1 pint boiling water*
> *2 tsp soy sauce*
> *2 tbs brown sugar*
> *pinch salt*
>
> *120g/4oz rice noodles*
>
> *Set the oven to 170°C(325°F)/ Gas mark 3*

1.

Peel the carrots. Cut them into slices about ½cm (¼in) thick. Then cut each slice in half.

2.

Cut the ends off the spring onions. Slanting your knife, cut them into 4cm (2in) sections.

3.

Wipe the mushrooms with damp kitchen paper. Trim the stems and cut a cross in the tops.

Wedge of leaves

4.

Roll the cabbage leaves up into a parcel. Slice through each parcel to make wedges of leaves.

5.

Peel the potato. Cut it into slices ½cm (¼in) thick. Cut the tofu into 2cm (1in) cubes.

6.

Dissolve the stock cube in the boiling water. Stir in the soy sauce, sugar and salt.

7.

Arrange each vegetable in a group around a casserole dish. Add the noodles in a group too.

8.

Pour on the stock and cook your casserole with the lid on for about 45 minutes.

Japanese meals

The dishes of a Japanese meal are all put onto a low table at the same time. People sit on cushions on the floor to eat with chopsticks. (See how to use them on page 39).

Sushi snacks

Sushi are parcels of raw fish and rice, often wrapped in dried seaweed. Sushi are served as starters, or as a takeaway snack from cafés in Japan called 'sushi bars'. Sushi chefs train for years to make them exactly the right way.

Rice

In Japan, rice is so important that the Japanese word for rice, 'gohan', also means food. Cook about 60g (2oz) of long grain rice for each person. Follow the instructions on the packet.

There is often a stylish flower arrangement on Japanese tables. Making them is an ancient art called 'ikebana'.

Dipping sauce

The Japanese often dip each piece of food from the main dish in a dipping sauce before they eat it. These sauces are put in a tiny bowl next to a person's chopsticks and eating bowl.

You will need:

6 tbs lemon juice
6 tbs soy sauce
1 tbs brown sugar

Mix the ingredients together in a bowl. Put the sauce in the refrigerator for as long as you can before pouring into saucers and serving it with your Japanese meal.

Set the table very simply, without cluttering it up. Each person needs a bowl and a spoon or chopsticks.

The art of arranging food is called 'moritsuke' in Japan.

Indonesia

Indonesia is made up of over 3,000 islands. They are famous for the spices that grow there. For centuries, people called them The Spice Islands.

Chicken in coconut sauce

More coconuts grow in Indonesia than anywhere else in the world, so cooks there use them a lot. They add a creamy taste to this chicken dish. Try serving it with plain boiled rice.

You will need:

4 chicken breasts
3 tbs vegetable oil
2 onions, chopped
3 cloves of garlic, peeled and crushed

60g/2oz cream of coconut (most supermarkets sell it)
300ml/½ pint hot water
1 tbs lemon juice
1 tsp ground ginger
1 tsp chilli powder
pinch salt and pepper

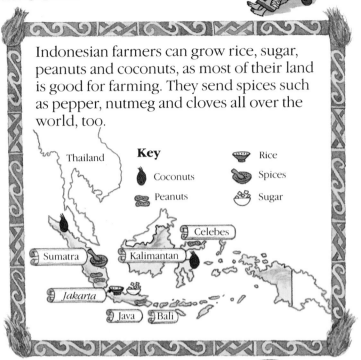

Indonesian farmers can grow rice, sugar, peanuts and coconuts, as most of their land is good for farming. They send spices such as pepper, nutmeg and cloves all over the world, too.

Thailand

Key

Coconuts
Peanuts
Rice
Spices
Sugar

Sumatra
Kalimantan
Celebes
Jakarta
Java
Bali

1.
Heat the oil in a large frying pan. Gently lower the chicken breasts into it. Cook them for about five minutes on each side.

2.
Lift the chicken breasts out onto some kitchen paper. Sprinkle them with the ginger, chilli powder, salt, pepper and lemon juice.

3.
Fry the onions and garlic until they are soft. In a bowl, dissolve the creamed coconut in the hot water to make a thin, white milk.

4.
Put the chicken back into the pan and pour the coconut milk over the top. Cook the dish over a low heat for about 40 minutes.

Indonesian food is often beautifully presented. Try decorating your dish with a sprig of mint or a wedge of lemon.

Smelly fruit

This fruit, called the durian fruit, is very popular in Indonesia. It smells like rotten cheese but tastes like sweet custard, people say.

Australia and New Zealand

The original people in Australia were called Aborigines, and Maoris first lived in New Zealand. In the 1700s, European convicts were sent there, far from home, as a punishment. They planted crops from Europe, and cooking here is now a mixture of traditional and European styles.

Lamingtons

These cakes were named after an Australian politician called Bruce Lamington. They are now popular in Australia and New Zealand.

You will need:

250g/8oz butter or margarine	*120g/4oz icing sugar*
180g/6oz caster sugar	*1 tbs cocoa*
250g/8oz self-raising flour	*2 tbs warm water*
2 eggs	*90g/3oz desiccated coconut*
6 tbs milk	
1 tsp vanilla essence	*Set the oven to 170°C (325°F)/ Gas mark 3*

A lot of Australia and New Zealand is wild land called the bush. No-one lives there. Farmers keep sheep and grow fruit, and grapes for wine on the good land.

Key: Cattle, Citrus fruit, Grapes, Sheep, Wheat

Australia — Sydney — Melbourne — Wellington — New Zealand

1. Put the butter and sugar in a bowl. Use a wooden spoon to mix them together until they are smooth and creamy.

2. In another bowl, whisk the eggs with a fork. Beat them into the butter mixture bit by bit. Stir in the milk and vanilla essence.

3. Sieve the flour into a bowl. Add it to the mixture by making gentle slicing movements with a metal spoon. Do not stir hard.

Use a tin 18 x 28cm (7 x 11in) and 4cm (1½in) deep.

4. Grease and line a baking tray. Tip in the mixture and smooth the top. Bake for 25-30 minutes, until golden brown.

Beach barbecue

Barbecues are a speciality of Australia and New Zealand. The sunny climate is ideal for cooking outside. Christmas Day there is in mid-summer, so Christmas lunch is often a barbecue on the beach.

5. Let the cake cool, then cut it into 7cm (3in) squares. Lift each square out onto a wire rack to cool down.

6. Sieve the icing sugar and cocoa into a bowl. Mix in the water for a smooth, runny paste that drops from a spoon as you count three.

7. Using a metal spoon, spread icing onto the top of each square. Let it drip down the sides. Sprinkle with coconut.

Jewish cooking

Jewish people live in many countries of the world. Their religion has strict laws about how food is prepared. When cooks follow these rules, the food they make is called kosher, which means 'suitable'. Jewish recipes vary slightly from country to country, as cooks adapt them to what food is available. You do not need to be Jewish, or know their rules, to enjoy these two dishes.

Cheesecake

Jewish cheesecake is usually baked in an oven, cooled, then chilled in a refrigerator. It takes a bit of time to make, but is a delicious pudding.

You will need:

10 digestive biscuits
90g/3oz butter or margarine
375g/12oz cream cheese or curd cheese
3 eggs, separated (see page 5)
90g/3oz caster sugar

6 tbs lemon juice
150ml/¼ pint double cream

 Set the oven to 180°C(350°F)/Gas mark 4

1.

Put the biscuits into a clean plastic bag. Roll a rolling pin over the bag until the biscuits are crumbs.

2.

Melt the butter in a pan. Off the heat, stir in the crumbs. Make sure the butter is well mixed in.

Round, metal tin with loose bottom.

3.

Pour the mixture into a 20cm (8in) greased cake tin. Press it flat with the back of a spoon. Bake it for ten minutes.

4.

Beat together the cheese and egg yolks. Add the sugar, cream and lemon juice and beat again.

A long wait

Cheesecake reminds Jews of their prophet Moses, they say. He waited so long for God to tell him the rules of their faith that milk had time to turn into cheese.

This takes a few minutes.

5.

Whisk the egg whites until they form soft, peak shapes when you pull blobs up with the end of your whisk.

6.

Making cutting movements with a metal spoon, gently add the egg whites to the creamy mixture.

7.

Pour the mixture into the crumb case and cook for 45-50 minutes until firm. Let it cool, then remove from the tin (stand it on an upturned bowl and draw the outside 'wall' down). Chill for an hour in the refrigerator.

Potato latkes

These crispy potato cakes are called latkes. They are delicious hot, straight after cooking, or served cold with some sour cream and salad. This recipe makes ten latkes.

You will need:

4 medium-sized potatoes
1 small onion

1 egg
pinch salt
and pepper
3 tbs vegetable
oil

The water stops it going brown.

1.

Peel and then grate the potatoes. Put the grated potato into a bowl of cold water straight away.

2.

Peel and grate the onion. In a bowl, beat the egg with a fork. Add the onion, salt and pepper and beat again.

3.

Tip the grated potato into a sieve and shake off any water. Add it to the egg mixture and stir well.

⚠️

4.

Heat the oil in a frying pan. Put tablespoonfuls of mixture into the pan and press them flat.

5.

Fry each latke for about five minutes on each side. Lift them onto kitchen paper and serve straight away.

Jewish bread

In most countries where Jews live, shops sell kosher food for them to eat. Jewish bakeries sell several sorts of kosher bread, cakes and biscuits. Here are three of them.

This is a bagel. Bagels are delicious served sliced in half and filled with smoked salmon and cream cheese.

This plaited bread is called challah. It is baked specially for Jewish festivals.

These biscuits are called matzos. They are often crumbled into soups or made into dumplings called matzo balls.

Index

The words which appear in *italics* are things which you can buy as part of a meal. They are not things to make.